Zoe and the Beam

Chapter 1

Zoe loved doing gymnastics.

Her father said that she had started doing gymnastics when she was 14 months old.

He had left her laying on the couch while he was in the kitchen. Then he heard a plop!

When he ran to the couch her father found Zoe face down in the carpet.

He thought she had fallen off the couch, so he put her back on the couch and tucked her in with pillows around her.

As soon as he turned his back -plop! Zoe was face down in the carpet again.

She had jumped off the couch!

She kept jumping off the couch over and over. Then she started climbing everything she could find.

The stairs were easy. Then, at two years old, she climbed across the railing high above the stairs. Zoe's mother was going to cry out, but her father put his fingers to his lips and said "Don't teach her fear."

When Zoe climbed to the top of the highest climbing net in town, at three years old, even her father was unsure.

Now, at eight years old, she hoped that, one day, she would compete at the Olympic Games.

So Zoe trained hard.

She loved doing flic flacs and back tucks
on the floor.

She loved doing giants on the bar.

She loved doing front layouts on the vault.

But most of all she loved the beam.

For her beam competition, she had to press up to hold a handstand and then come back down.

She had to go backwards and forwards to do a tic toc.

Then she had to jump high in the air to do
the splits and land back on the beam.

It all had to look beautiful and she couldn't fall off.

When Zoe was on the beam, it looked beautiful.

Zoe hardly ever fell off.

Chapter 2

At home Zoe also had a little practice beam.

It wasn't high. It just sat straight on the lounge floor.

One day her father said, "Zoe, I want you to try walking across the beam with your eyes closed. It will help your balance."

Zoe thought it would be easy.

But, it was hard.

She tipped one way, then the other.

She fell off.

Finally, she got across.

"See how many you can do in-a-row," her father asked.

Zoe could do three and no more.

On days that she wasn't training at her gymnastics club, her father would get the beam out.

Zoe passed three and five-in-a-row. It felt easier. She felt happier.

Then came eight times-in-a-row.

For three days she always fell before doing eight, no matter how hard she tried.

She got very angry and jumped off the beam, falling on the stairs in tears.

"That's okay to feel that," said her father. "But, remember, it's just the monkey mind playing tricks."

Zoe lifted her head up and smiled.

When she got back on the beam, her father said, "Breathe deep, down to your tummy. Stand straight, like you're hanging by a thread. Feel your feet sink into the beam."

Five, six, seven, eight! She did eight, nine, ten...twenty times, before she lost her balance.

With practice, Zoe soon could make it one hundred and fifty times across the beam without falling off.

Zoe felt happy.

Chapter 3

One night, when it was time to do the beam, Zoe suddenly felt tired.

Her shoulders slumped. She lay on the couch and yawned.

Her father said that she sounded like a cartoon animal when she spoke.

"Monkey mind," said her Dad. "Do one hundred and seventy times across."

Zoe started and fell off a couple of times.

Then she got into a rhythm. She sped along the beam.

"Slow down," called her father.

She kept speeding. "Slow down!" called her father.

Finally, with thirty to go, she did slow down.

It was easy...very easy.
Zoe felt relaxed.
What a wonderful feeling.

Zoe finished and hugged her father. "I love you," she said.

Zoe had thought that her father had meant her body being balanced.

Now she knew that he really meant her mind being balanced.

She had learned how important it was to have a balanced, quiet mind.

Zoe loved the beam, more than ever.

Zoe's guide to balancing mind and body on the beam

Read this carefully. This is something that you don't get taught in school – or even at gymnastics clubs…all of us kids have a monkey mind.

Okay, you might think that I'm cuckoo but check it out yourself…

If some of these sound like you then you have a monkey mind:

Monkey mind hops from one idea to another – it can't keep still.

Monkey mind often chatters and chatters.

Monkey mind doesn't like being told what to do – even by parents and coaches.

Monkey mind can't stick with learning something at school or sports, it wanders off the task.

Monkey mind tells you to do the wrong thing even when you know what's right.

Can you guess what to do with your monkey mind?

How to calm your monkey mind by balancing your mind and body.

This is like walking a tight-rope with your eyes closed. It helped me to get a balanced and quiet mind.

For gymnasts: It also helped me to get great balance for the beam and not fall off even when doing fantastic things. It could help you do fantastic things too.

STEP 1

Ask your parents if you may do this first! Find something narrow, about the size of three quarters of an adult hand, to walk along. If you have a wooden floor you could use a floorboard, as wide as a beam.

: Get your mum or dad to get a piece of wood and cover it in vinyl. The wood should be 10 cm (4 in) wide, not too thick and at least 275 cms (9 ft) long (not too long that someone can't carry it though).

Important!

Make sure the area around your beam is clear of chairs and tables in case you lose your balance – when I started I lost my balance a lot. Have your mum or dad watch to count how many times that you walk the beam and to remind you about things that will help you balance.

STEP 2

Stand on the end of the beam ready to do slow steps forward.

STEP 3

Close your eyes and breathe deep into your stomach.

STEP 4

Slowly take steps forward and keep breathing deeply into your stomach.

STEP 5

Once you feel the end of the beam or piece of wood open your eyes.

STEP 6

Turn around and do it again. See how many times you can walk the beam without losing balance or falling off (I had trouble doing even 3 times in-a-row when I started).

STEP 7

Walk the beam - with your eyes closed - twice a week or more. Try to do more times walking the beam without losing balance each time.

My monkey mind got me angry, sad and tired sometimes because it didn't want me telling it what to do. Yours might too – if this happens get a parent to help you keep walking the beam by reminding you that your monkey mind is playing tricks.

It took me eight weeks to be able to do it 170 times in-a-row without losing balance.

My monkey mind was really calm and well behaved then. I felt great! You can too!

TIP 1

Keep your head and chin level – not pointing down.

TIP 2

Imagine that there is a string joined to the top of your head that holds you up and lets you step lightly on the beam.

TIP 3

Feel your feet – what does the beam feel like under your feet? Make sure your feet always step in the middle of the beam and are straight.

TIP 4

Don't take the next step before you have good balance.

TIP 5

Relax - always relax.

TIP 6

Keep practising – don't give up!